INSPIRATIONAL LIVES

# NELSON MANDELA
## REVOLUTIONARY PRESIDENT

### Kay Barnham

WAYLAND

Published in paperback in 2016
First published in hardback in 2014
Copyright © Wayland 2014

Wayland
An imprint of
Hachette Children's Group
Part of Hodder & Stoughton
Carmelite House
50 Victoria Embankment
London EC4Y 0DZ

Editor: Hayley Fairhead
Design: Basement68
Picture Research: Shelley Noronha

A catalogue record for this title is
available from the British Library.

968'.065'092-dc23
ISBN: 978 0 7502 9311 2
Library ebook ISBN: 978 0 7502 8788 3

Printed in China

An Hachette UK company
www.hachette.co.uk
www.hachettechildrens.co.uk

Picture acknowledgements:
The author and publisher would like
to thank the following for allowing
their pictures to be reproduced in this
publication: Cover: © Rex Features;
p4 © Newscom/Photoshot; p5
© Stephane De Sakutin/AFP/Getty
Images; p6 © Susan Winters Cook
/Getty Images; p7 © Sipa Press/Rex;
p8 © Africa Media Online/Mary Evans;
p9 © Sipa Press/Rex; p10 © IDAF/Rex;
p11 © Gallo Images/Alamy; p12
© Bettmann/Corbis; p13 © Times
Newspaper/ Rex; p14 © UPPA/
Photoshot; p15 © UPPA/Photoshot;
p16 © Shutterstock.com; p17 © Sipa
Press/ Rex; p18 © Ron Mitchell/
Associated News/ Rex; p19 © AP/Topham;
p20 © Richard Young/ Rex; p21 © Anna
Zieminski/ AFP/Getty Images; p22 ©
Alexander Joe/AFP/Getty Images; p23 ©
Walter Dhladhla/AFP/Getty Images;
p24 © Walter Dhladhla/AFP/Getty
Images; p25 © Jean-Pierre Muller/AFP/
Getty Images; p26 © AFP/Getty Images;
p27 © Andrew Winning/Reuters/Corbis;
p28 © Foto24/Herman Verwey/Rex;
p29 © Istockphoto.com.

# Contents

# The fight for equality

'Today the world lost one of the true giants of the past century. Nelson Mandela was a man of incomparable honour, unconquerable strength, and unyielding resolve – a saint to many, a hero to all who treasure **liberty**, **freedom** and the **dignity** of humankind.'
Oscar-winning actor Morgan Freeman on hearing the news of Nelson Mandela's death.

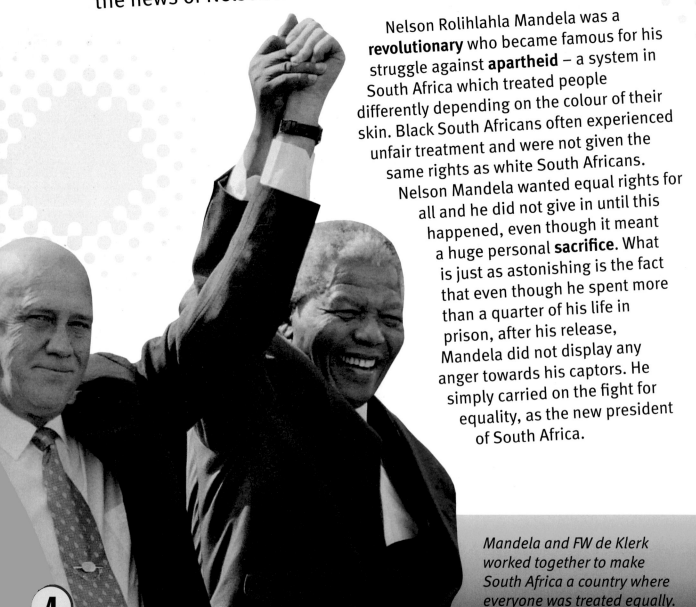

Nelson Rolihlahla Mandela was a **revolutionary** who became famous for his struggle against **apartheid** – a system in South Africa which treated people differently depending on the colour of their skin. Black South Africans often experienced unfair treatment and were not given the same rights as white South Africans. Nelson Mandela wanted equal rights for all and he did not give in until this happened, even though it meant a huge personal **sacrifice**. What is just as astonishing is the fact that even though he spent more than a quarter of his life in prison, after his release, Mandela did not display any anger towards his captors. He simply carried on the fight for equality, as the new president of South Africa.

*Mandela and FW de Klerk worked together to make South Africa a country where everyone was treated equally.*

Mandela was an inspirational person throughout his life: when he and the African National Congress (ANC) fought against apartheid; when he was behind bars; and when he was the South African president. Mandela died on 5 December 2013 and the memorials and **tributes** flooded in.

*'He was renowned the world over as the undisputed **icon** of forgiveness and **reconciliation**, and everybody wanted a piece of him. We South Africans basked in his reflected glory.'*
Archbishop Desmond Tutu

*'He worked tirelessly for the good of his country, and his **legacy** is the peaceful South Africa we see today.'*
Queen Elizabeth II

This book follows Nelson Mandela's story. Discover where he was from, where he lived and what he did to be remembered as such a great man throughout the world. Find out the real story behind the man who changed South Africa.

*Nelson Mandela lived from 1918 to 2013. He was an inspiration to young and old during his lifetime.*

## HONOURS BOARD
### Awards and achievements:
Mandela received over 250 awards during his lifetime, but the most famous was the Nobel Peace Prize, which he shared with the man who released him from prison, FW de Klerk, in 1993.

# The boy from Mvezo

Rolihlahla Mandela was born in Mvezo, a small village in South Africa, in 1918. His great-grandfather was king of the Thembu tribe and his father was a local chief. This meant that traditional **customs** and **rituals** were very important as Mandela grew up.

Mandela's father – Nkosi Mphakanyiswa Gadla Mandela – had four wives and thirteen children. Mandela grew up in the village of Qunu with his mother – Nonqaphi Nosekeni – and two sisters. He spent much of his time outdoors, looking after herds of cows and playing with other children. At the age of seven, he became the first person in his family to go to school. There, he was given the English name 'Nelson' by his teacher.

Mandela's father worked as a **counsellor** for the royal family. After he died, twelve-year-old Mandela went to live with the Thembu royal family. King Jongintaba treated him like a son.

*Only a few hundred people live in Mvezo, the village where Mandela was born.*

Mandela continued his education near his new palace home. There, he studied English, his native Xhosa language and geography. But his favourite subject was history and he loved learning about his South African **heritage**.

He went on to boarding school, college and then university, meeting people from different backgrounds. Among the many new friends he made was Oliver Tambo, a person who would be very important in Mandela's future.

Even though he knew members of the African National Congress (ANC), Mandela did not join this political party at university. But he and Tambo showed they could stand up for what they believed in when they took part in a student protest. Unfortunately, their involvement meant that they were both expelled from university.

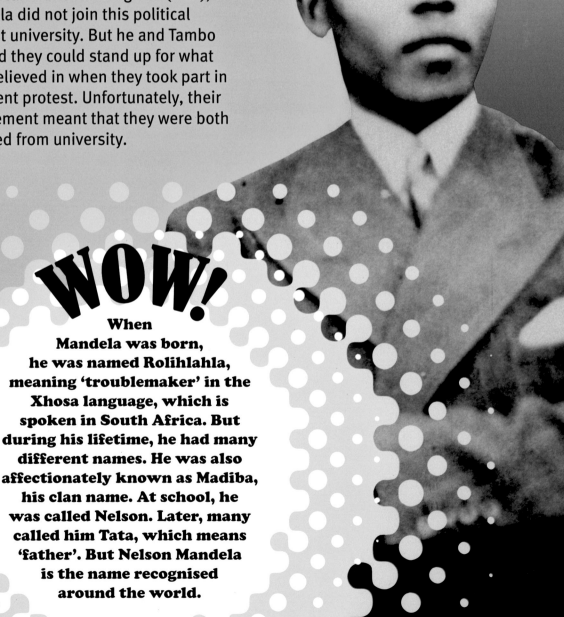

*In 1937, Mandela went to college in Fort Beaufort, before studying for a degree at Fort Hare University.*

# WOW!

When Mandela was born, he was named Rolihlahla, meaning 'troublemaker' in the Xhosa language, which is spoken in South Africa. But during his lifetime, he had many different names. He was also affectionately known as Madiba, his clan name. At school, he was called Nelson. Later, many called him Tata, which means 'father'. But Nelson Mandela is the name recognised around the world.

# The runaway

When Mandela returned home from university without finishing his degree, the king was furious with him. But worse was to come. King Jongintaba arranged a marriage for him. This was something that Mandela really didn't want and when he found out, he ran away to Johannesburg. What he saw there shocked him.

Black and white people were made to live apart. Certain areas of public places were reserved for white people. Meanwhile, black people were forced to live in **townships** – areas built at the edge of towns and cities. Here, they suffered extreme poverty, terrible living conditions, pollution and crime. Black people did not have the same rights as white people: they weren't allowed to move freely; they weren't even allowed to vote in normal elections. These rules later became known as apartheid.

Mandela found a job as a night watchman at a gold mine, but when those in charge found out that he was a runaway, he was fired. Luckily, he met Walter Sisulu who found Mandela a job at a law firm instead. There, he studied law.

During the 1950s it was decided that some areas would be white-only; black people were evicted and taken with their belongings to black townships.

# INSPIRATION

The African National Congress, or ANC, is a political party. When the ANC was formed in 1912, black and white people in South Africa were treated very differently and kept apart. Then and now, the ANC's aim is to bring all Africans together as one people.

Meanwhile, Mandela had joined the ANC, like Walter Sisulu and his old friend Oliver Tambo. He helped to form the ANC Youth League, in which he played more and more important roles, becoming secretary and eventually president.

It was because of Sisulu and the ANC that Mandela met Evelyn Ntoko Mase. A trainee nurse, she was one of Sisulu's relatives and an ANC member. Evelyn and Mandela were married in 1944 and had four children together.

## WOW!

When he wasn't working or studying or being involved in ANC activities, Mandela enjoyed dancing, boxing and long-distance running.

*Mandela liked the fact that during a boxing match, a person's colour was not important.*

# The political activist

The National Party was a political party run by white **Afrikaners**. After they won the election in 1948, apartheid became law. Non-white South Africans had to learn, live and travel separately. They could not even visit the same doctors or go to the same beaches as white people.

Mandela was against apartheid, but he was against violence too. He thought that the best way to fight the new laws was with peaceful protests, such as **boycotts** and **strikes**. In 1950, he was elected as president of the ANC Youth League. The following year they launched their Defiance Campaign against Unjust Laws.

In 1952, Mandela was speaking to a rally of 10,000 people in Durban, telling them how the ANC planned to oppose apartheid with more protests, when he was arrested and put in prison. It was the first time he'd been to prison, but it wouldn't be the last.

In 1953, the law firm 'Mandela and Tambo' opened for business.

## INSPIRATION

'Mandela and Tambo' was the first black legal firm in South Africa. It was very popular. The two friends helped many black people, offering them cheap or even free legal services.

Mandela was soon released and moved up the ranks in the ANC, becoming the president of the Transvaal region. Meanwhile, membership of the ANC grew. A month later, Mandela was arrested again. This time, he was charged and then found guilty of **communism**. However, his sentence for hard labour was suspended and he was set free. But it was becoming more and more difficult for Mandela to take part in ANC activities. He was banned by the authorities from ANC meetings and from public speaking too.

Then in 1956, Mandela and many other important members of the ANC were arrested and charged with **treason** for plotting against the state. In 1961, after a trial lasting a long four and a half years, he was declared not guilty.

Meanwhile, Mandela's private life was full of drama too. In 1958 Mandela and Evelyn divorced and he married a social worker named Winnie Madikizela.

## WOW!

It took Mandela many years to be awarded with his own law degree. He was so busy with his ANC activities that he failed many of the courses that he took. He also admitted that he wasn't a very good student!

*Mandela met Winnie Madikizela at a bus stop! They were married for 38 years and had two daughters together.*

# A change of heart

Although Mandela had once believed in non-violence, his views changed after the events of 21 March 1960 in a township called Sharpeville. On that day, a **demonstration** was held in which thousands protested against the **pass laws** – a type of passport system that stopped black people moving freely within South Africa. Police fired upon the crowds of unarmed black **protestors**, killing 69 people and injuring 180.

The Sharpeville **Massacre** shocked South Africans. Afterwards, there were strikes, protests and riots. A state of emergency was declared, thousands of people, including Mandela, were arrested and the ANC was banned.

The events shocked people around the world. There were demonstrations in many countries about apartheid. International governments and businesses began to turn their backs on South Africa, in protest at the way black people were being treated.

## INSPIRATION

In South Africa, 21 March is now commemorated as **Human Rights** Day, to remember those who died in the Sharpeville Massacre. The United Nations Educational, Scientific and Cultural Organisation (UNESCO) marks the date as the International Day for the Elimination of Racial Discrimination.

*Many victims of the Sharpeville Massacre were shot in the back, showing that they were running away from the police when they were fired upon.*

Mandela went into hiding. He no longer believed that peaceful protest would work. When the new military side of the ANC was formed, he became its leader. They attacked power supplies and government buildings to get their message across.

Using the name David Motsamayi, Mandela left South Africa illegally in 1962. He went to gather support for the ANC's campaign throughout Africa and also to receive military training. But on his return, he was arrested and charged with leaving the country without a passport.

He was back in court, again.

**WOW!**

While he was in hiding during the 1960s, Mandela disguised himself as a chauffeur, a gardener and a chef. He evaded capture so many times that he became known as the Black Pimpernel, named after the Scarlet Pimpernel –a fictional hero with a secret identity.

*Back in 1952, Mandela had burned his pass book in protest at the pass laws.*

# Guilty!

This time, Mandela did not escape jail. Found guilty of encouraging workers to strike and leaving the country without a passport, he was sentenced to five years' hard labour in South Africa's notoriously tough prison on Robben Island.

Worse was to come. A year after Mandela was sentenced, police raided a farmhouse in Rivonia, where leaders of the ANC were holding a secret meeting. When the police found evidence that they were planning **sabotage** and **guerrilla warfare**, the men were arrested. And, even though he was in prison, Mandela's name was found on some paperwork, which meant that he was seen to be involved too.

Mandela was now in big trouble. If found guilty of sabotage, he and the others could face the death penalty.

The Rivonia Trial received a lot of publicity, not just in South Africa, but in other countries too. Around the world, people were starting to take more and more notice of apartheid in South Africa.

*Police guard the Supreme Court in Pretoria during the Rivonia Trial.*

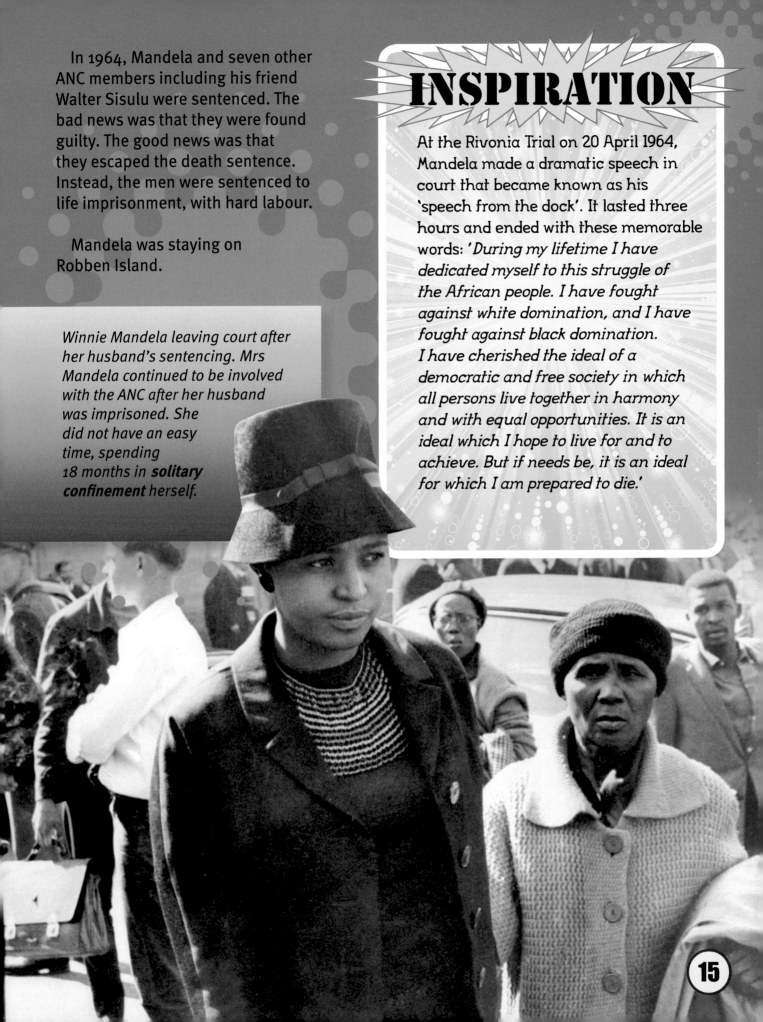

In 1964, Mandela and seven other ANC members including his friend Walter Sisulu were sentenced. The bad news was that they were found guilty. The good news was that they escaped the death sentence. Instead, the men were sentenced to life imprisonment, with hard labour.

Mandela was staying on Robben Island.

*Winnie Mandela leaving court after her husband's sentencing. Mrs Mandela continued to be involved with the ANC after her husband was imprisoned. She did not have an easy time, spending 18 months in **solitary confinement** herself.*

# INSPIRATION

At the Rivonia Trial on 20 April 1964, Mandela made a dramatic speech in court that became known as his 'speech from the dock'. It lasted three hours and ended with these memorable words: *'During my lifetime I have dedicated myself to this struggle of the African people. I have fought against white domination, and I have fought against black domination. I have cherished the ideal of a democratic and free society in which all persons live together in harmony and with equal opportunities. It is an ideal which I hope to live for and to achieve. But if needs be, it is an ideal for which I am prepared to die.'*

# An island prison

Robben Island sits in the Atlantic Ocean, 7km from the Cape Town coastline. The tiny, rocky island is just 3.3km long and 1.9km wide. With its dangerous shoreline, it's the scene of many shipwrecks. It was also once the home of South Africa's maximum-security prison. And it was where Mandela spent 18 years of his life.

Life on Robben Island was tough. Mandela's concrete cell measured just 2.4 metres by 2.1 metres. There was no bed. Instead, he slept on a straw mat. And the toilet was a bucket. Later, Mandela blamed the damp conditions in his cell for the **tuberculosis** he received treatment for in 1988.

*Robben Island sits a few kilometres away from the South African mainland. It was a remote and isolated home for the prisoners.*

## WOW!

On Robben Island, the one highlight of the week for the prisoners was film night, which was every Thursday. Mandela grew to love films.

Mandela wasn't just locked up. He and the other political prisoners were sentenced to hard labour and on Robben Island this meant smashing rocks into tiny pieces. It was back-breaking work.

After a year, the prisoners began work in a limestone quarry. Here, they chipped lime from the rock face, then broke it into smaller pieces. But the conditions here were even tougher. The prisoners breathed in limestone dust, damaging their lungs. Meanwhile, when the sun shone brightly, the light reflecting from the limestone was blinding. Mandela's eyes were permanently damaged from the glare.

It wasn't just the prisoners' bodies that suffered – they suffered in other ways too. Mail was **censored**. Newspapers were banned. And when his mother died in 1968 and his son Thembi was killed in a car accident in 1969, Mandela was not allowed to leave the prison to go to their funerals. His wife Winnie could only visit once every six months.

But he refused to give up hope and Mandela became the leader of the other political prisoners on Robben Island.

# INSPIRATION

These are the words that US president Barack Obama wrote in the guest book on Robben Island, when he visited in 2013. *'On behalf of our family, we're deeply humbled to stand where men of such courage faced down injustice and refused to yield. The world is grateful for the heroes of Robben Island, who remind us that no shackles or cells can match the strength of the human spirit.'*

In this photo from 1964, prisoners on Robben Island can be seen breaking bigger rocks into smaller ones and sewing prison clothes.

# A powerful symbol

It was now illegal even to talk about Mandela in South Africa. The ANC was outlawed. Yet, even though he couldn't speak to his supporters, Mandela had become a symbol for the struggle for freedom. And worldwide support for the anti-apartheid movement was growing.

President Botha and his government were under pressure from countries around the world to release Mandela and put an end to apartheid. Foreign companies stopped doing business with South Africa, banks stopped investing and South African foods were boycotted.

Sporting events were disrupted by apartheid too. South Africa would not allow teams of both black and white players to compete. Other countries protested by refusing to play against South Africa. Athletics, cricket, golf, Formula One, rugby union, football and tennis were affected. South Africa was even banned from the International Olympic Committee in 1970.

The South African government refused to ban apartheid. But the international pressure didn't stop and neither did the black **activists** in South Africa who continued their protests.

*Anti-apartheid rallies were held in London in the 1980s.*

In 1982, Mandela left Robben Island. He was not free, but he was moved to Pollsmoor Prison in Cape Town. Here, the conditions were better.

In 1985, President Botha offered to give Mandela his freedom. But there was a condition. Mandela would only be released if he promised to speak out against violence by black activists. In his reply – read out by his daughter Zindzi to a huge crowd in Jabulani Stadium, Soweto – Mandela turned down Botha's offer. He wanted full **democracy** or nothing.

# WOW!

**While in prison, Mandela carried on his studies by post, working towards a degree with the University of London.**

# INSPIRATION

'I cherish my own freedom dearly, but I care even more for your freedom... Only free men can **negotiate**. Prisoners cannot enter into contracts... I cannot and will not give any undertaking at a time when I and you, the people, are not free. Your freedom and mine cannot be separated. I will return.'

Nelson Mandela's words from the Jabulani Stadium speech, February 1985.

*Mandela's daughter Zindzi read out a letter from her father in which he refused President Botha's offer of conditional freedom.*

# Free Nelson Mandela

Mandela remained in prison. But, in 1984, a band called The Special A.K.A. released a track that boosted his international fame even more. *Nelson Mandela* was a protest against his imprisonment. Later, it also became known as *Free Nelson Mandela* and was a huge hit in South Africa and around the world.

In 1988, Mandela celebrated his 70th birthday, in jail. But earlier that year, his birthday was celebrated in a much more public way, when a tribute concert was held in London to call, yet again, for his release.

Thousands of people packed into Wembley Stadium to watch artists such as Sting, Tracy Chapman, George Michael, Stevie Wonder, Simple Minds, UB40, The Bee Gees, Peter Gabriel, Eurythmics and Jerry Dammers (who wrote the track *Nelson Mandela*) perform. Oscar-winning actors Richard Attenborough and Whoopi Goldberg gave rousing speeches.

But Mandela was not freed.

*At the Nelson Mandela 70th Birthday Tribute concert, 74,000 people watched in Wembley Stadium.*

## WOW!

Mandela's birthday concert was televised in 67 countries around the world and was watched by 600 million viewers!

However, after being treated for tuberculosis in late 1988, he was moved to Victor Verster Prison near Paarl. His new home was a world away from the dank cell on Robben Island. Now he lived in a warder's house, had his own cook and was allowed many visitors. He was able now to send messages to his old ANC friend, Oliver Tambo.

*Nelson Mandela goes back to visit his house in Victor Verster Prison. He experienced much better living conditions here compared to those on Robben Island.*

Then President Botha became ill and had to step down as president. He was replaced by FW de Klerk. The new president decided that apartheid could not continue and made the surprise move of setting free all ANC prisoners... except one.

Mandela was *still* not free.

Many members of the South African government did not want Mandela to be released. But de Klerk was determined. He discussed the situation with his government. He discussed it with Mandela himself, and at long last came the news that people around the world had been waiting for.

After 27 years in prison, Mandela was *free*.

# The 'Walk to Freedom'

There were no conditions attached to Mandela's release from prison. He could say what he liked, do what he liked and support whichever party he wanted, because the ANC was now no longer banned.
He was totally free.

On 11 February 1990, after 27 years of captivity, Mandela left Victor Verster Prison with his wife Winnie. Crowds of overjoyed supporters were there to meet him. They cheered as a smiling Mandela raised his fist high in a victory salute, a free man at last. The historic moment was televised live around the world.

After shaking hands with his supporters, Mandela and his wife were driven to Cape Town. At City Hall, they were met by even bigger crowds. Everyone was eager to hear what he had to say and Mandela didn't disappoint.

*Mandela's first steps away from the prison became known as his 'Walk to Freedom'. This inspired the title of his autobiography, which told of his struggle against apartheid – Long Walk to Freedom (Little, Brown Book Goup, 1994).*

He thanked everyone who had campaigned for his release. Among the many people and organisations he saluted were the people of Cape Town, Oliver Tambo and the ANC. He greeted the people of his country, religious communities, traditional leaders, young people, his wife, family and many others besides.

'Today, the majority of South Africans, black and white, recognise that apartheid has no future,' Mandela said. 'The destruction caused by apartheid on our subcontinent is **incalculable**.'

Mandela stressed how he was a loyal member of the ANC and agreed with their aims. He said that the need to unite everyone in South Africa was as important as ever. He praised de Klerk for his efforts so far, but said that now the government and the ANC needed to discuss an end to apartheid and a democratic future, together.

# INSPIRATION

*'Our march to freedom is irreversible. We must not allow fear to stand in our way. Universal **suffrage** on a common voters' role in a united democratic and non-racial South Africa is the only way to peace and racial harmony.'*
Mandela, Cape Town, 11 February 1990

*When he was released from prison, Mandela forgot to bring his glasses with him. So when he gave his speech to crowds in Cape Town, he had to borrow Winnie's glasses to read the words!*

# President Mandela

In 1991, Mandela became the president of the ANC. Meanwhile, he was in the middle of talks with President de Klerk. They worked so hard to bring about a peaceful end to apartheid and towards democracy in South Africa that the two men were awarded the Nobel Peace Prize in 1993.

By 1994, Mandela and de Klerk had helped the leading parties to agree that all citizens could vote, not just the white South Africans. The country went to the polls, 23 million people voted and the ANC won. However, they did not win enough votes to be totally in charge. The ANC would have to work with the other parties to form a government. But there was no argument over who would be South Africa's new leader. It was, of course, Nelson Mandela.

When Mandela became president in 1994, he said: '...we shall build a society in which all South Africans, both black and white, will be able to walk tall without any fear in their hearts, assured of the **inalienable** right to human dignity, a rainbow nation at peace with itself and the world.'

## WOW!

Mandela was a film star too! He made a brief appearance in the film *Malcolm X* (1992), the true story of another human rights activist. He played a schoolteacher and read out one of Malcolm X's speeches.

For Mandela, one of the most important tasks of his presidency was to bring different races together. He wanted South Africa to be a 'rainbow nation'. As the new Deputy President, FW de Klerk was a member of his new cabinet, along with other members of the National Party.

But even though Mandela wanted to make sure black South Africans had a fair deal, he didn't want to alienate white South Africans as he did so.

During apartheid, the Springboks – the South African rugby team – had only white players. This made black South Africans very angry. But at the Rugby World Cup final in 1995 in Johannesburg, Mandela arrived at the game wearing a Springboks' shirt and cap. He won the hearts of white South Africans. Then the Springboks' went on to win the match and the Rugby World Cup.

*When Springboks' captain Francois Pienaar saw Mandela wearing his number, he had felt so emotional that he could not sing the national anthem.*

# A new South Africa

When Mandela became president, South Africa was a country with many problems: more than half of the population did not have electricity; a third of the population was unemployed; the country was in debt; and even though some were wealthy, poverty was widespread. The new leader had a lot to do.

While he was in power, Mandela's government made improvements to welfare, healthcare, education, water and electricity supplies, communications, workers' rights, land rights and housing.

Even though he had been a prisoner for so many years, Mandela did not want revenge and he encouraged others who had suffered to 'forget the past' too. Instead, they should concern themselves with the present and the future, he said.

*Archbishop Desmond Tutu was the chairman of the Truth and Reconciliation Commission. The commission was set up so that those responsible for apartheid could apologise to their victims.*

## INSPIRATION

'If you want to make peace with your enemy you have to work with your enemy. Then he becomes your partner.' *Long Walk to Freedom* by Nelson Mandela (1994)

People who had committed **racist** violence under apartheid were not prosecuted. Instead, they met the victims and their families, to explain what had happened and to apologise. Then they heard how the victims and their families had been affected by the crimes. It was the first time anything like this had happened and while some people around the world were shocked, others, like US president Bill Clinton, applauded Mandela's idea.

Mandela always said that he would only do one term in office and he was as good as his word. After five years as South African president, he stepped down and then spent his time working for charities instead, raising millions.

In 1995, Mandela and his wife Winnie divorced, though they remained friends. On his 80th birthday, Mandela married Graça Machel, the widow of Mozambique's president.

*Mandela's HIV and AIDS charity was named after his prison number: 46664.*

46664
It's in our hands

# A giant of history

When Mandela died on 5 December 2013 at the age of 95, South Africans mourned 'the father of the nation'. Tributes and praise flooded in from all around the world for 'Madiba'.

His memorial service was held five days later at the FNB Stadium in Johannesburg and was attended by world leaders, royals, celebrities and tens of thousands of South Africans. It was broadcast live on televisions around the world. And even though it rained heavily, people sang, chanted and danced in celebration of Nelson Rolihlahla Mandela's life and achievements.

In his speech at the memorial, US president Obama said, 'To the people of South Africa – people of every race and every walk of life – the world thanks you for sharing Nelson Mandela with us... a giant of history, who moved a nation toward justice, and in the process moved billions around the world.'

US president Obama called Mandela 'a giant of history'.

## WOW!

Nelson Mandela International Day is celebrated on 18 July, which was Mandela's birthday. It is a day to 'bring together people around the world to fight poverty and promote peace and reconciliation'.

Ten days after his death, Mandela was buried on a hill in Qunu, the village where he grew up and once herded animals. Both his wife Graça and his ex-wife Winnie were at his graveside after a ceremony that included sermons, speeches, hymns, funny stories about Mandela, a military fly-past and the *Last Post*.

When Nelson Rolihlahla Mandela was born in 1918, black South Africans had few rights. They could not move freely, they could not vote and they had to work in mines or on farms. In the twenty-first century, thanks to the efforts of Mandela and many, many others, South Africa is a very different place where black and white people live together peacefully in a 'rainbow nation'.

# INSPIRATION

While on Robben Island, Mandela was inspired by the poem *Invictus* by Victorian poet William Ernest Henley. He read it aloud to other prisoners to inspire them too. It ends with the empowering words...
*'I am the master of my fate:
I am the captain of my soul.'*

*Nelson Mandela attends the unveiling of a statue of himself in London, in 2007. His struggle for freedom inspired people across the world.*

# Have you got what it takes to be a revolutionary leader?

**1) If you see that something is unfair, do you try to change it?**
a) What's the point? Nothing I can say or do will change anything.
b) If other people are trying to change something, I'll help.
c) Yes. I'm not afraid to try and make a difference.

**2) Do you enjoy meeting new people?**
a) Not really. I've got my best friends and I stick with them.
b) I feel shy when meeting new people, but I try to make an effort.
c) I love meeting new people! Bring it on.

**3) Are you good at confrontation?**
a) No. I'll do anything to avoid an argument.
b) I'll argue my corner if I have to, but sometimes it's just easier to agree with the other person's point of view.
c) Oh, yes. I always say what I think.

**4) Are you good at public speaking?**
a) No way. I prefer to talk to one or two people at a time, not crowds.
b) I suppose that I don't mind talking in front of the class...
c) It doesn't bother me whether I'm talking to one person or three hundred. It's just important for me to get my point across.

**5) Are you good at forgiving people?**
a) No. I've got a memory like an elephant. If someone's done something to upset me, I never forget. And I never forgive.
b) Sometimes. It depends what they've done wrong.
c) Of course. What's the point in holding a grudge?

**6) Are you determined to succeed, no matter how long it takes?**
a) If something can't be done in five minutes, I'm not interested.
b) Yes, but I get bored if things take too long to achieve.
c) Absolutely. I never give up.

## RESULTS

**Mostly As**: You're too cautious and you give up too easily. You're probably not the right person to lead a revolution right now. Try to be a bit more determined.

**Mostly Bs**: You're heading in the right direction, but you're not there yet. Stand up for what you believe in and you might just get there.

**Mostly Cs**: You're just the sort of person Mandela would have admired: fair, confident, forthright, determined, and you find it easy to forgive. Keep going and one day you might change the world!

# Glossary

**Activist**  Someone who tries to force political or social change.

**Afrikaner**  A white person from South Africa who speaks Afrikaans, often descended from Dutch people.

**Apartheid**  A system in South Africa that treated people differently depending on the colour of their skin.

**Boycott**  To avoid doing business with someone as a form of punishment.

**Censored**  To remove information.

**Communism**  A political idea where everyone shares a nation's wealth equally.

**Conditional**  Something with conditions attached.

**Counsellor**  Advisor.

**Customs**  Traditions.

**Democracy**  When a government is voted for by the country's people.

**Demonstration**  When lots of people take to the streets to complain.

**Dignity**  Being respected.

**Freedom**  To do as you like.

**Guerrilla warfare**  Unofficial military action by small groups of people.

**Heritage**  Traditions and history.

**Human rights**  The respect and rights that every person deserves.

**Icon**  A person who is highly respected and may stand for something.

**Inalienable**  Something that you cannot take away from someone.

**Incalculable**  Something that is impossible to work out.

**Legacy**  What someone leaves behind when they die.

**Liberty**  Freedom.

**Massacre**  When a number of people are killed violently.

**Negotiate**  To discuss something and come to an agreement.

**Pass laws**  A type of passport system that stopped black people moving freely within South Africa.

**Protestor**  Someone who objects to something, loudly and in public.

**Racist (adj)**  Someone who judges another by the colour of their skin or by their nationality.

**Reconciliation**  The process of forgiveness.

**Revolutionary**  Someone who wants to overthrow a government.

**Rituals**  Special ceremonies.

**Sabotage**  The deliberate disruption of something.

**Sacrifice**  To give up something important.

**Solitary confinement**  Being imprisoned alone.

**Strike**  To refuse to work unless conditions are met.

**Suffrage**  The right to vote.

**Township**  Areas built at the edge of towns and cities that were reserved for black people.

**Treason**  The crime of betraying your country.

**Tribute**  To show thanks and admiration.

**Tuberculosis**  A serious lung disease.

# Index